WESTCOAST FLOWERS

An Adult Coloring Book to Inspire Your Soul

Diana Ng

R.N., B.SC.N., M.A.

KaDa PUBLISHING

Library and Archives Canada Cataloguing in Publication

Ng, Diana, Author

WESTCOAST FLOWERS: An Adult Coloring Book to Inspire Your Soul

Diana Ng, R.N., B.Sc.N., M.A.

Issued in print and electronic formats.   ISBN 978-0-9939379-5-8 (PDF)

Published in Canada by KaDa Publishing

Printed in Canada

First edition

Introduction

Welcome to my Westcoast Flower Coloring Book!

I created this coloring book from my love of nature—beaches, gardens, and mountains—for its reverent beauty, soothing properties, and healing powers.

Each time I walk, hike, or stroll in our natural environment, I receive the same reliable effects—of inner peace, stillness, and wonder, which I hope to spread to you.

May the process of coloring these floral pictures feed your soul.

Enjoy!

The Scribble Page

Let us be grateful to the people who make us happy;
they are the charming gardeners who make our souls blossom.

—Marcel Proust

Daisies

By appreciation, we make excellence in others our own property.

—Voltaire

Magnolias

Make the most of yourself for that is all there is of you.

—Ralph Waldo Emerson

Clematis

Let yourself be silently drawn by the strange pull of what you really love. It will not lead you astray.

—Rumi

Tulips

The mind is everything; what you think, you become.

—**Buddha**

Daffodils

What lies behind us and what lies before us are small matters compared to what lies within us.

—Ralph Waldo Emerson

Roses

Life without love is like a tree without blossoms or fruit.

—Khalil Gibran

Peonies

Peace begins with a smile.

—Mother Teresa

Sunflowers

Be who you are and say what you feel
Because those who mind don't matter
And those who matter don't mind.

—Dr. Seuss

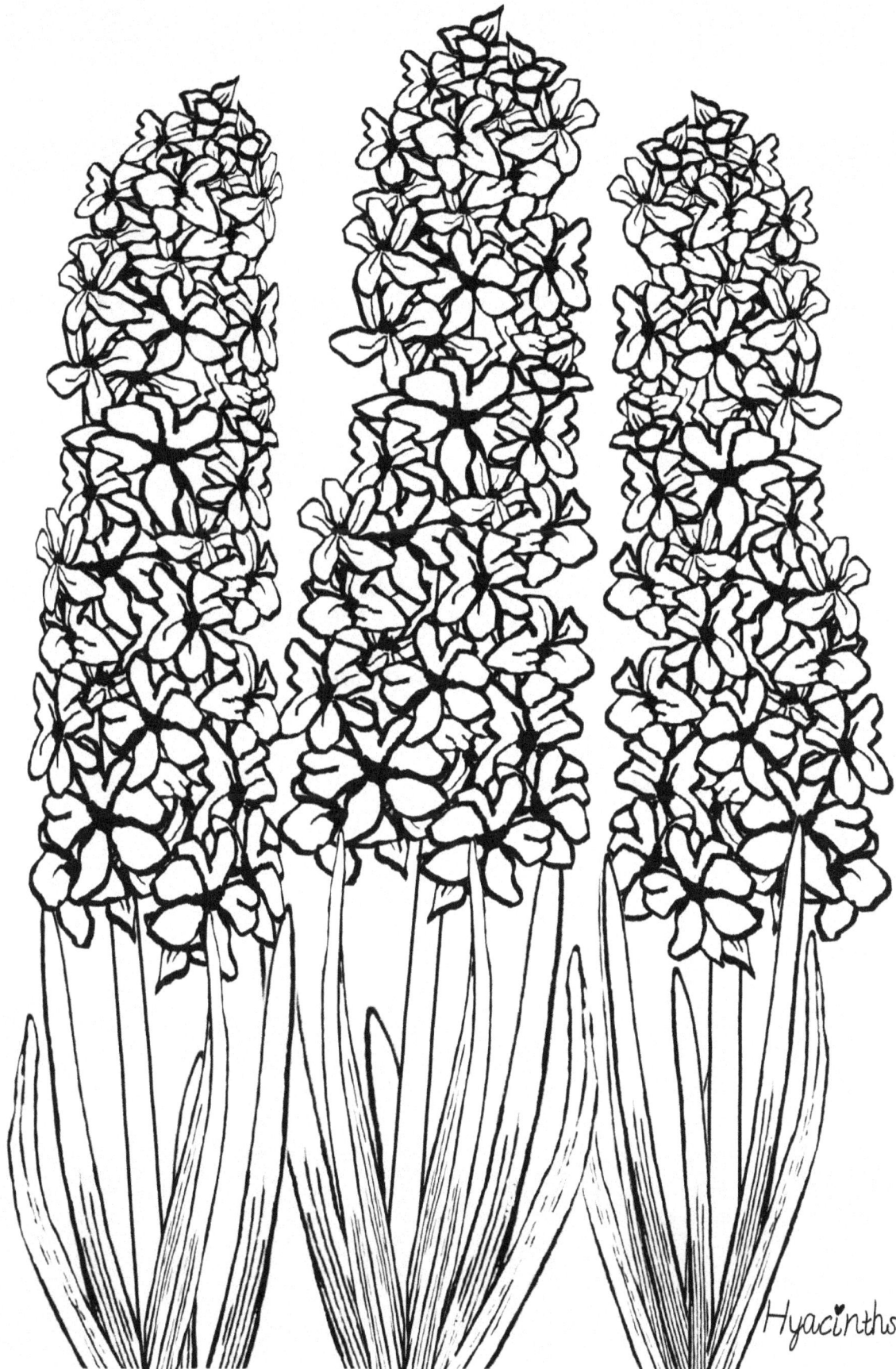

Hyacinths

The lotus springs from the mud.

—Chinese Proverb

Water Lilies

Gratitude is the sign of noble souls.

—**Aesop**

Alliums

To thine own self be true.

—William Shakespeare

Petunias

Bloom where you are planted.

—Unknown

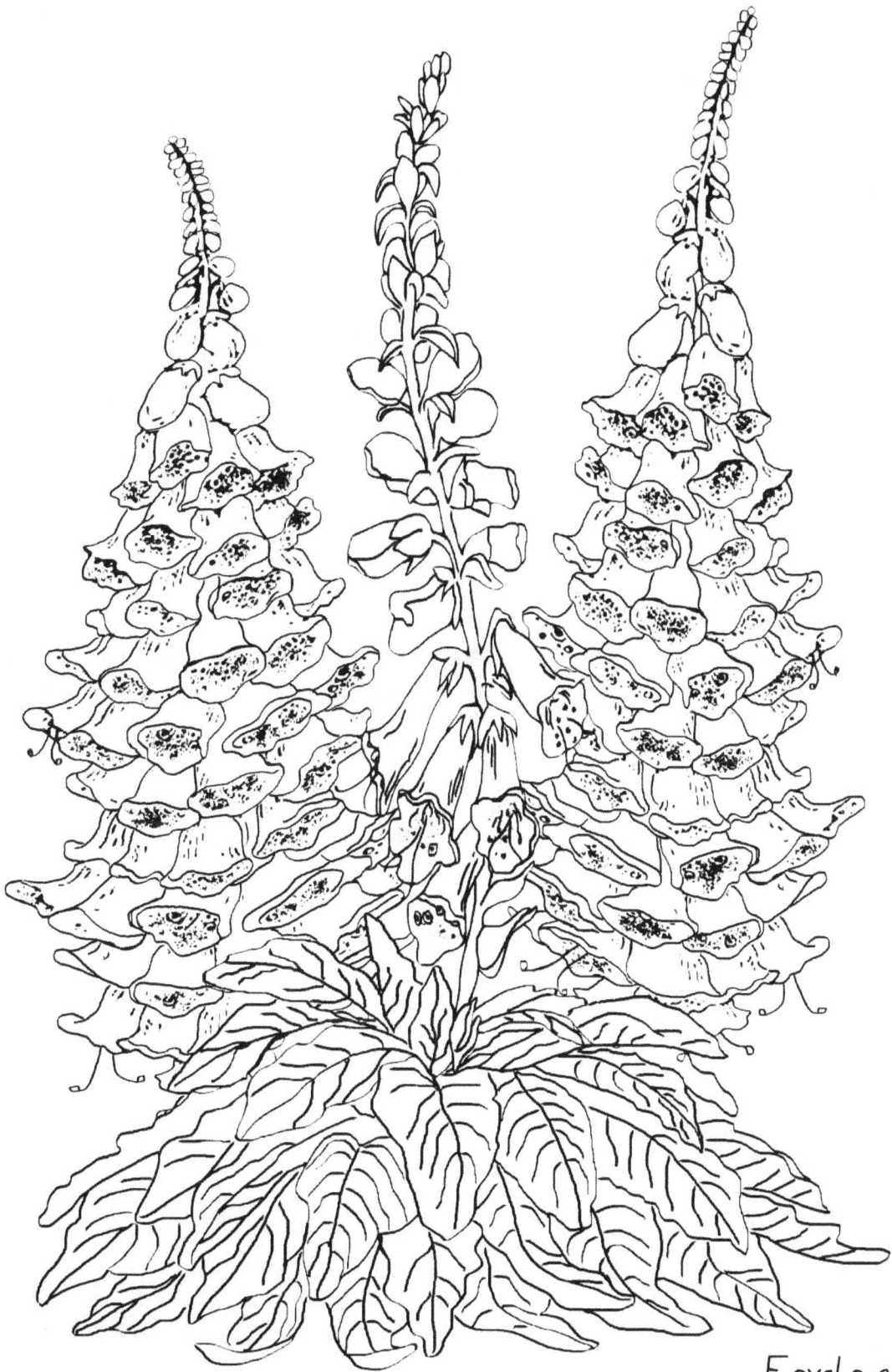

Foxgloves

Do not spoil what you have by desiring what you have not; but remember that what you now have was once among the things only hoped for.

—Epicurus

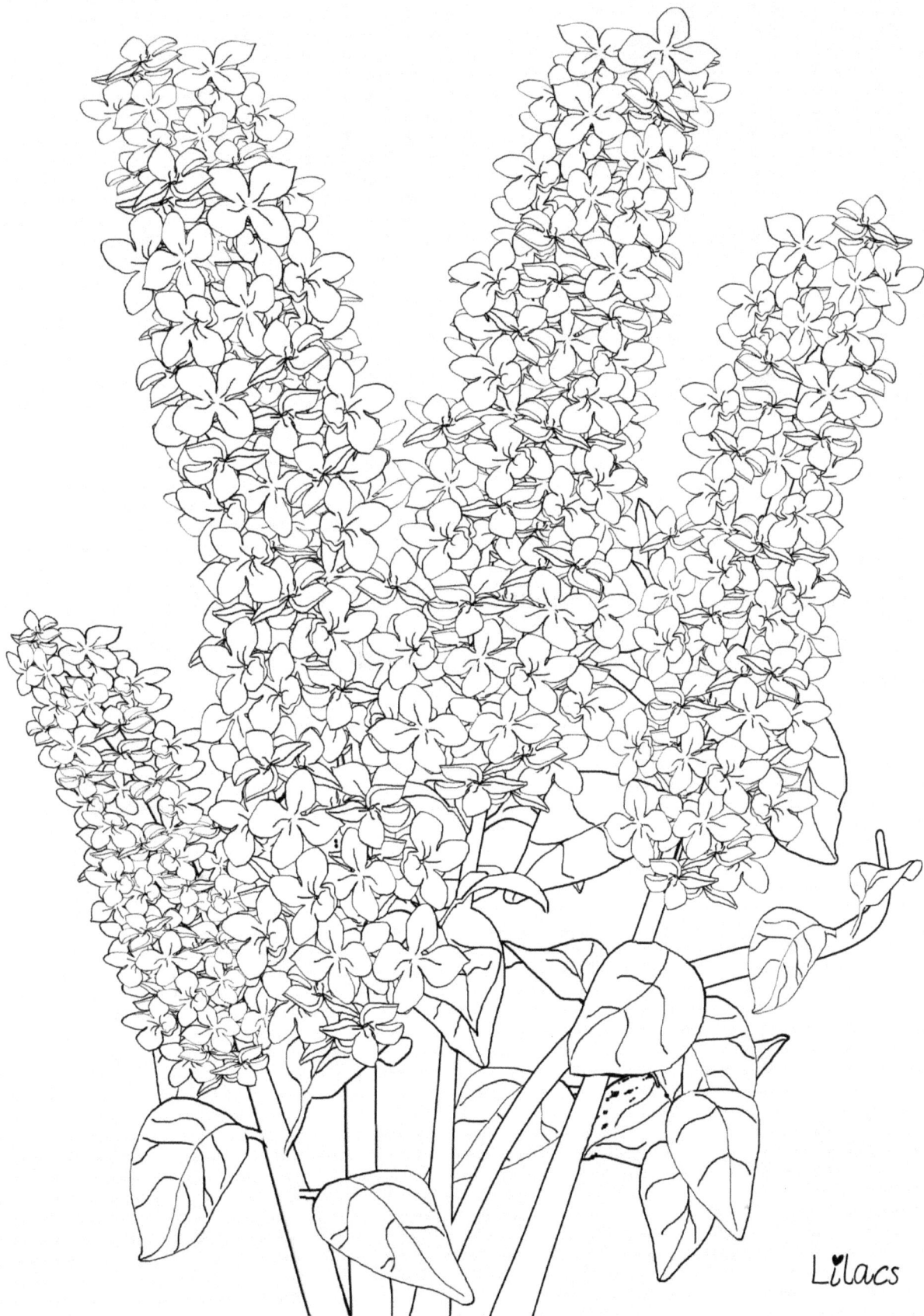
Lilacs

Gratitude is the fairest blossom which springs from the soul.

—Henry Ward Beecher

Honeysuckles

A garden is always a series of losses set against a few triumphs,
like life itself.

—May Sarton

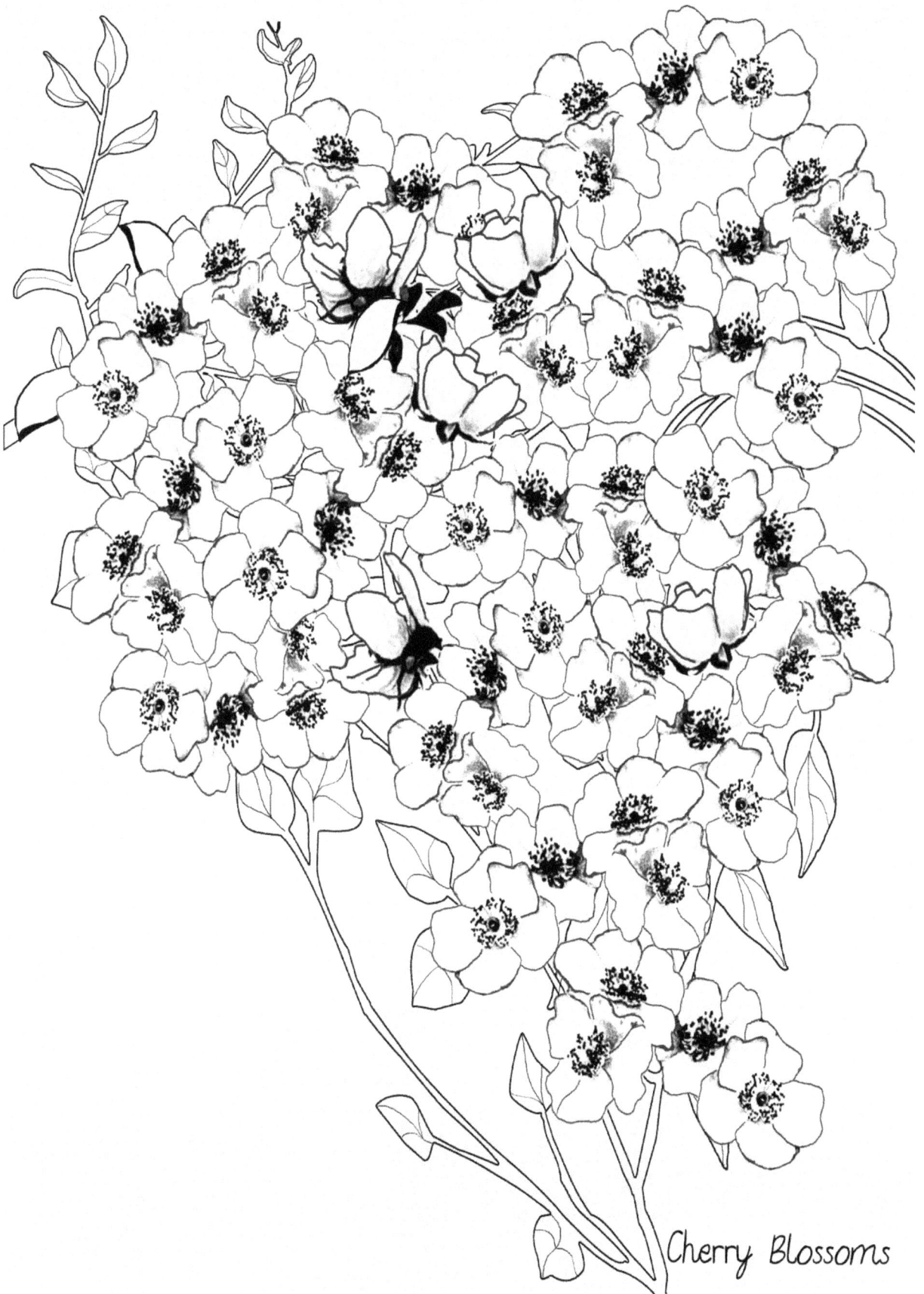

Cherry Blossoms

Gratitude is not only the greatest of virtues, but the parent of all others.

—Marcus Tullius Cicero

Azaleas

A friend is one who overlooks your broken fence and admires the flower in your garden.

—Unknown

Fuchsias

Peace comes from within. Do not seek it without.

—**Buddha**

Lavenders

Flowers leave some of their fragrance
In the hand that bestows them.

—Chinese proverb

Hydrangeas

Friends are flowers in the garden of life.

—Proverb

Geraniums

There is always music amongst the trees in the garden, but our hearts must be very quiet to hear it.

—Minnie Aumonier

Rhododendrons

Hem your blessings with thankfulness so they don't unravel.

—Author Unknown

Passionflowers

Everything grows better with love.

—Unknown

Wisteria

Turn your face to the sun and
the shadows will fall behind you.

—**Maori Proverb**

Dahlias

Wake at dawn with a winged heart and give thanks for another day of loving.

—Kahlil Gibran

Reflections

May the sun

bring you new energy by day,

May the moon

softly restore you by night,

May the rain

wash away your worries,

May the breeze

blow new strength into your being,

May you walk

gently through the world and know

its beauty all the days of your life.

—Apache Blessing

. . .

**Diana Ng appreciates you leaving a review
of this coloring book on Amazon.**

For other unique, exquisite gifts for mindfulness and meditation,
visit Diana's online peace store
http://www.labyrinthlady.ca/peacestore

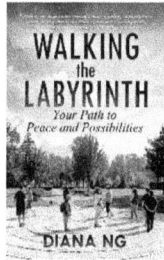

Watch for our soon to be released gorgeous labyrinth necklace to match our elegant labyrinth earrings!

Join our newsletter for updates: http://labyrinthlady.ca

About the Author

Diana Ng, R.N., B.Sc.N., M.A., is a Leadership Consultant with a nursing background; she worked for over twenty years in health promotions and postsecondary education. Currently, she is an International Speaker and Consultant encouraging openness, equality, and collaborative leadership in organizations. She is recognized by her community as the Labyrinth Lady.

Need to decrease stress or develop leadership in your organization? Have a problem in your workplace that is becoming unmanageable? Need solutions to enhance morale, productivity, and collaboration in your company?

Call (+1) 604–765–7493 or email diana@labyrinthlady.ca to schedule a complimentary consultation.

Visit her website: www.labyrinthlady.ca

You can also connect with Diana on social media:

www.facebook.com/vancouverlabyrinth

www.twitter.com/diana_ng

www.linkedin.com/in/ngdiana

www.plus.google.com/+DianaNglabyrinth

www.pinterest.com/vanlabyrinth

www.instagram.com/vancouverlabyrinth

www.youtube.com/channel/UCXvM5jbQzJ79reUa-lej7Ew

www.ingramcontent.com/pod-product-compliance
Lightning Source LLC
Chambersburg PA
CBHW081723270326
41933CB00017B/3280